ANNE

A Life from Beginning to End

Copyright © 2019 by Hourly History.

All rights reserved.

Table of Contents

Introduction
Early Life as a Lady-in-waiting
The Curse of a King
Anne Boleyn at Court
The Rise of the Boleyns
Making Way for a New Queen
The King's Great Matter
Anne Ascends the Throne
Another Birth, Another Tragedy
Trial and Execution
Conclusion

Introduction

Anne Boleyn is most likely the best-known of Henry VIII's six wives; she is also the most controversial. History has represented Anne as either a whore or a martyr. The true story, however, is far more complex.

When discussing subjects such as Anne Boleyn, it is best to remember that history is written by the victors. After Anne's execution following an outrageous sham trial, Henry VIII and his men tried to remove any trace of her. During a period when every high-ranked person was having his or her portrait painted by famed artists, including all of Henry's other wives, no contemporary reproduction of Anne Boleyn remains. Similarly, her love letters to Henry were destroyed. It was more convenient for Henry VIII to pretend his second wife had never existed.

But exist she did. When joining Queen Catherine's ladies-in-waiting at the English court, Anne made an instant splash. The king noticed her immediately. Henry's decades-long marriage to Catherine was at this point disintegrating rapidly as the queen had been unable to provide him with the son and heir he so desperately needed to secure the Tudor line. Anne, however, rejected Henry's offer to become his mistress out of hand. At both the French and English court, she had witnessed royal mistresses ruined and tossed aside. This was not to be her fate.

The more Anne resisted, the more Henry pursued her. The only way for him to beget an heir was to have his marriage to Catherine annulled and marry a younger, more fertile woman. It took seven years for him to accomplish this goal—years which involved wowing Anne and separating his country and church from Rome and the pope's authority.

Although Henry probably fancied Anne, her sole purpose as his wife was to produce an heir. When Anne failed to give birth to a son, Henry's solution was simple: get rid of her and marry a new woman. At her trial, the woman who had most likely been a virgin when she married the king was accused of having taken half a dozen lovers, including her own brother. She was called a witch and a whore. Anne's guilty verdict and execution happened so quickly, even she was surprised to be taken from her jail cell one morning and escorted to the gallows. Her death had to happen straight away before anyone came to their senses. Anne Boleyn died as she had lived, with dignity and without apology.

Chapter One

Early Life as a Lady-in-waiting

"She knew perfectly how to sing and dance."

—Lancelot de Carles about Anne Boleyn

Anne Boleyn's birth date is unrecorded, but she is believed to have been born around 1505. Her father, Sir Thomas Boleyn, was one of the new Renaissance men who had successfully worked his way up the social ladder even though he was a vocal advocate of the new reformed religion making its way from Germany. Thomas was smart and loyal and became a trusted diplomat for England's King Henry VIII. He was well-rewarded for his services, and the Boleyns lived a comfortable life in their country manor, Hever. They weren't a part of the true royal circle, but they were well-respected.

The Boleyn family's successful ascent in society included making several advantageous marriages. Thomas himself had married Lady Elizabeth Howard, a member of the powerful Howard family. They had three children, with Anne being the middle child. She had an older sister, Mary, and a younger brother, George. Thomas was determined to see his daughters well-educated. This was an unusually progressive attitude for the times. Anne, although the younger girl, stood out with her intelligence and natural wit. At around the age of six, Anne was sent to the French court to serve Queen Claude, the wife of King Francis I. Her sister Mary followed a few years later.

Being sent to the French court for social training was a customary way of acquiring poise and preparing well-heeled English daughters to rise at court and gain favorable marriages. The French court was the most cultured court in the world and visited by the most learned people. Anne was eager to make a good match, and this was the perfect place to be groomed.

French society was dazzling and opened up a new world for the Boleyn sisters. Queen Claude demanded a high standard of behavior from her ladies, and Anne readily complied. She dutifully learned proper needlepointing, singing, and dancing. She met important people from around the world and learned to captivate a crowd with her charm. No one ever described Anne as a great beauty, but she learned to dazzle men with her poise and wit.

Although Anne was popular, she did not engage in any romance. Her sister Mary, on the other hand, became the mistress of the womanizing King Francis, who soon discarded her to his courtiers. Mary quickly gained a reputation as the "great whore" while enjoying the perks of the French court. It appears that Mary's goal was to have fun, while Anne wanted to learn as much as possible.

Mary's antics were an embarrassment to Sir Thomas, who hurried to call his older daughter back to England before she could cause any more damage. In London, Mary was placed as a lady-in-waiting to Queen Catherine and immediately found herself in bed with King Henry VIII.

No two sisters could have been more different. While Mary romped her way from one bed to another, Anne avoided romantic entanglements. Mary was oblivious to her reputation, while Anne guarded hers like a treasured jewel. Anne's future actions suggest that she had paid attention to her sister's behavior and was determined not to repeat Mary's mistakes.

Around the age of 20, Sir Thomas called Anne back to England, where she, like her sister, served Queen Catherine. Anne made an immediate impression at court. After years in France, she had developed a sophistication and elegance few English girls could match. Her wardrobe, chic and Parisienne, stood out. She was quickly surrounded by admirers, including the poet Thomas Wyatt.

King Henry noticed her the moment she appeared in court, despite the fact that he was still having an affair with her sister Mary. That little detail didn't stop Henry from pursuing Anne at the same time. Anne politely spurned his advances. King Henry, who had never been denied anything in his life, only became more ardent in his pursuit. Anne ignored him as best as she could. She wanted a husband, and she had seen what happened to royal mistresses, who invariably were discarded and forgotten.

Her instincts would prove correct. Like Francis, Henry soon tired of Mary, even though Mary had most likely borne him two children whom he never acknowledged as his. In the end, Mary married a lowly lord and was disowned by her family and banished from court. She lived out her life on the countryside in obscurity. This was not for Anne. She did not intend to become any man's reject, even if that man was the king of England.

Anne's brother George worked in the king's bedchamber, so she had to tread carefully between refusing Henry and not infuriating him enough to have him punish her family. She perfected a mating dance that kept the king at a safe distance while preventing him from becoming angry. These were social rituals she had perfected at the French court, playing coy without making any definitive promises. Henry only grew more enchanted.

Anne's only near-romance was with Henry Percy, son of the Earl of Northumberland. They planned on getting married even though Percy was already promised to another lady. Cardinal Thomas Wolsey, King Henry's closest advisor, thought marriage to Anne would be beneath Percy, and nothing more came of the discussions.

When the king began to threaten her many male admirers, Anne removed herself several times from court and returned to the safety of Hever. Perhaps this was at the request of her father, who had already seen one daughter ruined.

But Henry was relentless. He could have had, and had had, any woman he wanted at the snap of a finger. No one refused the king. He visited Anne in Hever with promises and even sent her the gift of a deer he had killed. The symbolism could not have been clearer: he was the hunter; she was his prey. One of Henry's many letters and love songs dedicated to Anne read: *"I wolde you were in myne armes or I in yours for I think it long syns I kyst you"* ("I would you were in my arms or I in yours for I think it long since I kissed you") .

Anne rarely responded to Henry's florid prose. Finally, like an adolescent desperate for a prom date, he offered her the position of *maîtresse en titre*, the French title of a king's chief mistress. This was certainly a remarkable offer from Henry, and one many women would have grasped at. But to his dismay, a lovelorn Henry learned that Anne Boleyn was not like any other woman.

Chapter Two
The Curse of a King

"Whoever leads an auspicious life here and governs the commonwealth rightly, as my most noble father did, who promoted all piety and banished all ignorance, has a most certain way to heaven."

—Edward VI, Henry VIII's son

By the time Henry VIII became besotted with Anne Boleyn, his marriage to Catherine of Aragon was already failing. After more than 12 years, Catherine still hadn't produced the son he desperately needed. Henry was a suspicious man; he began to think he was cursed for his sins and those of his father, Henry VII. And there were many sins which might have angered his God. Henry VIII's entire reign and marriage had been built on a series of lies and misdeeds. The truth was, the Tudor line had never had a strong claim to the throne of England. Was God punishing him by not giving him a son? The question tortured Henry.

Catherine, daughter of Isabella and Ferdinand of Spain, had arrived at the English court as a 14-year-old girl to become the wife of Henry's older brother, Arthur, bringing with her a generous dowry. The match was meant to bring an alliance between Spain and England and strengthen the Tudor claim to the throne via Catherine's prestigious

English ancestry. Arthur, who had always been weak and sickly, died a few months following the wedding, leaving behind a teenaged widow. Catherine had no intentions of returning to Spain, and Henry VII had no intentions of returning her dowry. For seven years, Catherine lived in a type of neverland, her future unclear. She was essentially a woman without a country, but she was determined to make her place in England.

Wily Henry VII finally suggested she marry his younger son, Henry. It was the perfect solution, but canon law forbade the marriage to one's brother's widow. So, Catherine insisted that her marriage with Arthur had never been consummated and was therefore not valid. In fact, the consummation of the marriage had been witnessed by many, as was the custom for royal marriages. But Catherine had inherited her mother Isabella's spine of steel. She never wavered from her story that she and Arthur had failed to consummate their marriage.

Based on her lie and a papal dispensation, Henry and Catherine were married in 1509. Henry was happy with his new queen at first. Catherine was known as a great beauty in her time. Tragically, throughout their marriage, she suffered half a dozen miscarriages and produced no male heir. Henry didn't consider his puny daughter, Mary, a viable successor. She was only a girl. As the years passed, the need for a son became dire.

Everyone knew that Henry VII had usurped the throne of England. Born in Wales, he had rarely even set foot in England prior to the Battle of Bosworth, where King Richard III met his final fate and Henry VII placed the crown of England on his own head, a crown to which he had no genuine claim. Henry VII was descendant from an illegitimate line born of an affair between Edward III son's John of Gaunt and Katherine Swynford, whom he eventually married. He legitimized their children, but legally and in writing, they were specifically excluded from any claim to the English throne. Margaret Beaufort, Henry VII's mother, was a member of that line of the family called the Lancasters.

On the paternal side of the family, Catherine of Valois, widow of Henry V, had married Welshman Owen Tudor, but the legitimacy of their son, Edmund, was questionable. Edmund Tudor married Margaret Beaufort, and Henry VII was their son. At the age of 14, Henry left Wales and lived in France for 13 years. This hardly placed him in line to become king of England.

It was Margaret, from the illegitimate Lancaster line, who urged her son to invade England and claim what she considered his birthright. But many Yorkists, the legitimate line to the throne, stood ahead of Henry's questionable claim. After he defeated Yorkist King Richard III, Henry VII killed or imprisoned as many Yorkists as possible. He spent his entire life paranoid about losing the crown which he had taken by force instead of by right. Some historians even believe he might have had a hand in the disappearance of the Princes in the Tower, Richard III's nephews.

His son, Henry VIII, was well aware of how fragile the Tudor line was. He could not claim legitimacy from either his paternal or maternal side. He, like his father, killed any possible opponents in an effort to remain in power. Fifty thousand people were executed during the reign of Henry VIII; he held his throne through sheer force of will. It was this lack of legitimacy to the crown of England that made the need for a legal son and heir so imperative. Without an heir, the Tudor line could very well end.

Even before Henry began to consider annulment from Catherine as his only option, he was casting an eye throughout Europe for another wife who could bear him a son. His chief minister, Cardinal Thomas Wolsey, was sent to search the continent for available and nubile princesses. At this point, Henry was desperate to replace his barren wife with another, but in his own mind, Anne was still only regarded as a potential mistress. Still, her continued refusals were unbearable to him. He had never been refused anything in his life, let alone a woman. Whether intentionally or not, Anne was driving him to distraction.

Chapter Three

Anne Boleyn at Court

"Her that set our country in a roar."

—Thomas Wyatt, poem about Anne Boleyn

At some point, Henry's view of Anne changed. After Anne sent him a statue of a bejewelled woman from Hever, he responded by sending her a letter which read, "The proofs of your affection are such, the fine posies of the letters so warmly couched, that they constrain me to ever to truly to honour, love, and serve you."

After seven years of conducting a delicate mating dance, Anne was showing a change of heart. The reason for this was simple. While Wolsey was still searching for another, suitable royal wife, Henry had asked Anne to marry him. It didn't matter whether she loved him. This was an offer no woman could refuse. Henry was known to be spiteful when slighted; he was like a child, expecting to have his demands met in all matters. Anne's entire family had worked diligently to rise in society. They would suffer the consequences if she refused a proposal of marriage.

Besides, her goal had been to make a brilliant match. In England, no match was more desirable than marriage to the king. They shared a mutual love of books and music and enjoyed a good discussion. They made an excellent couple. Anne must have considered herself a lucky woman—

except, of course, for the minor impediment of an already existing wife.

Anne was known for her intelligence, and Henry openly discussed what he considered the Tudor curse with her. Surely his marriage was devoid of a son because he had married his brother's wife. The marriage was illegal and against the will of God. He had sinned, and all he had to do was end his marriage to make things right. Divorce was out of the question, but Henry was counting on an annulment based on the canon laws. He was sure the pope would agree.

The entire Boleyn family, including Anne, were strong proponents of the new reformed religion, which strongly rejected the pope's dominance over other governments and rulers. There was an entire secret underground of reformists smuggling Martin Luther's writings from Germany into England. Sir Thomas Boleyn had many of these illegal and dangerous papers in his possession. This was, of course, considered treasonous. Anne, however, began to share these new doctrines with Henry. She gently attempted to persuade him that he was not at the mercy of the pope when it came to his marriage. This was news Henry was more than happy to accept. As he listened to Anne and these new, forbidden ideas, their relationship subtly shifted. He began to rely more and more on her for advice; Anne was telling him what he wanted to hear.

For Henry, this was an opportunity to rid himself of an unwanted wife. For Anne, it was the rare chance to openly advocate for the new religion in which she so strongly believed. This alliance brought them even closer together in a common purpose. Henry soon began to abandon most of his male companions as he spent more and more time in Anne's company. Lutheran writings were being circulated at court, and Anne saw it as her mission to spread the new learning.

Henry confessed his belief that his marriage was a sin to a group of learned ecclesiastical men at Westminster. He had hoped for their agreement. However, they refused to make a decision on the matter.

While they still didn't share a bed, Henry's intentions toward Anne were now public. She was his partner during an official reception for the French ambassador. She took part in political meetings and discussions. However, her initial appearance as Henry's betrothed was quickly followed by another retreat to the family estate, Hever. While Henry was working toward his annulment, they both agreed to remain circumspect about their relationship. Henry didn't want to give the pope any grounds for believing that the reason for the requested annulment was that he wanted another woman. He was making his argument on purely religious grounds that his marriage was invalid and sinful.

Henry visited Catherine at Windsor Castle and told her in no uncertain terms that they were no longer married. Not surprisingly, the stubborn and proud daughter of Isabella of Spain did not receive the news kindly. She had endured Henry's many other mistresses, and she assumed Anne was merely one of his passing fancies. Catherine raged that she wasn't one of his whores. Other discarded royal wives had been sent to a convent to live out their lives in obscurity. Catherine made it clear that she had no such intentions. She was queen, and she would remain so.

The obstinacy of his heretofore compliant wife infuriated Henry. He had miscalculated the meek manner wherein she had always shown him obedience. One way or another, he intended to have his way. However, Henry failed to take into consideration that Catherine still had a potent ace to play. She was the aunt of Charles V, the emperor of the Holy Roman Empire and one of the most powerful men in Europe. If Henry were going to prove victorious, victory would come at a price.

Chapter Four

The Rise of the Boleyns

"This passion of the King's is a most extraordinary thing. He sees nothing, he thinks of nothing but his Anne; he cannot be without her for an hour, and it moves one to pity to see how the King's life, the stability and downfall of the whole country, hang upon this one question."

—Campeggio

Anne still had not slept with Henry. Now that they were secretly betrothed, they both understood the need for caution. Her good reputation had to be maintained at all cost. Anne spent most of her time at Hever while Henry put together his case for an annulment. Even their letters had an air of restraint. Henry knew that his enemies, especially supporters of Catherine, would be only too happy to get their hands on them. Love letters between Henry and Anne would serve as proof in a court of law that Henry wanted an annulment because he was in lust, not because he felt guilt over marrying his brother's widow. The distinction was critical.

When Henry and Anne did spend time together in public, they made sure their movements were heavily chaperoned. No slurs and rumors were to circulate regarding Anne's behavior. Henry's chief minister, Cardinal Wolsey, knew of the king's infatuation with Anne.

He, like Catherine, assumed that Henry would soon tire of her, as he had of all his other mistresses. When Wolsey returned to England following his search for the perfect royal bride, he felt betrayed when he learned the truth. Henry and Anne were engaged. Why had he not been told?

To make matters worse, Anne was the daughter of Sir Thomas Boleyn, an adherent of the new religion and Wolsey's enemy. Wolsey had guided Henry since the king had been young. Now, the Boleyns were gaining favor at court, while his influence was clearly declining. The son of a butcher, Wolsey had risen to the highest level at court and had been Henry's main advisor for decades. The aristocracy considered him an upstart and loathed him. Wolsey realized that unless he took quick action, his days at court were numbered. As far as Wolsey was concerned, the sooner Anne Boleyn disappeared, the faster he would rise to full power once again.

Henry had already approached Pope Clement VII regarding his annulment. He was not anticipating any problems. Unfortunately for Henry, the pope's army had been invaded in 1527 by Emperor Charles V, Catherine's nephew. The pope was currently in hiding and cowering under the emperor's thumb. When a meeting with the pope was finally achieved, it was agreed that the pope's fellow cardinal Campeggio would go to England and join Wolsey. The two men were provided with a legal document authorizing them to handle the annulment on their own. That was the best the pope could offer.

The papal document was good news when the two men approached King Henry. However, it was soon discovered that the wording of the document effectively rendered it worthless. Pope Clement appears to have been too intimidated to incur the wrath of Charles V to allow the annulment to happen, and Charles V had no intentions of seeing his aunt discarded like yesterday's fish. Henry called out Wolsey in front of the entire court and publicly humiliated him for his failure.

A letter from Charles V to Henry made clear that all of Europe would rise in revolt if the annulment were to happen. Wolsey hoped this threat would be enough to put an end to this whole ugly matter. Henry went into a rage and refused to give up his engagement to Anne: "No other than God shall take her from me!"

At this particular time, the sweating sickness was making its way through England. Like the Black Plague a century earlier, it killed hundreds of people every day. Sanitary conditions were abominable, with horse and cow dung infiltrating the water supply. Fleas and bedbugs were everywhere, even in the best of households. Several of Henry's lords and servants perished from the illness. Fearful for his health, Henry left London immediately. However, at Hever, Anne fell ill. Henry quickly sent his own physician to look after her, and she soon recovered. The two were united once the danger had subsided, their meetings were taking place in the presence of Anne's mother.

By the end of 1528, Henry was able to elevate Anne's status at court. She no longer functioned as one of Queen Catherine's ladies, which was probably a relief to both women. Instead, Anne was given her own lavish household and attendant ladies and servants. Henry showered Anne with gifts of gold, diamonds, and furs. Nothing was too good for his future bride.

Anne used her new power, but not for herself. She used her influence with Henry to save as many members of the new reformed religion as possible. She also smuggled illegal English translations of the Bible from France to the reformists. To Henry, she pointed out a specific passage in *Obedience of a Christian Man* by reformist scholar William Tyndale: "Kings must make account of their doings only to God." These words were golden to Henry. Who needed the pope when all he had to do was go directly to God and ask for forgiveness for his sins? He became so enthralled with these new possibilities that he quickly pardoned a number of reformers. In his own mind, the annulment was now a mere formality. Anne would soon be his wife, and he would become the father of a healthy son and heir. The Tudor bloodline would be secured.

While Anne undoubtedly wanted to become queen, the ability to help spread the new religion gave her a sense of purpose. Her life now had real meaning besides belonging to a man, even if that man was the king. She was looking forward to her marriage with new assurance, as was Henry. The possibility of a break with Rome filled the king with excitement. It would solve all his problems. However, Henry, who had had his every wish granted since birth, was to find this more difficult than he had anticipated.

The role of Anne Boleyn in bringing Protestantism to England is not much known. But, in effect, she was the chief catalyst for the English Reformation. Henry's annulment from Catherine was of secondary consequence.

The primary event was England's break with Rome, which would be felt for generations to come.

Chapter Five

Making Way for a New Queen

"However displeasant it may be to the queen, truth and law must prevail."

—Archbishop Warham

With Anne kept conveniently out of the public's eye, Henry decided to take his case to a group of prelates and nobles. He argued that unless he had an heir, the country would be forced into another civil war, such as when the House of Lancaster had battled the House of York for three decades until his father's victory at Boswell. This conflict, known as the Wars of the Roses, was still a painful memory for many.

Henry made it clear that he had studied all the relevant scriptures and could only conclude that his marriage was a sin, punished by God. He also declared that since he sadly but necessarily considered his marriage to Catherine invalid, his young daughter Mary was as a consequence illegitimate and barred from taking the throne. Catherine, he assured everyone, was the gentlest and kindest of women. There was no fault in her, and he wished her nothing but well. If he were not barred by canon law from being married to her, he would certainly marry her again.

Needless to say, there was no mention of Anne in his speech. His words were reasonably well received. While some were still suspicious of his motives, Henry had made a good case for no longer wishing to live in sin.

Henry asked for a trial to settle the matter, but the pope's representative, Campeggio, delayed the opening. With the pope still afraid to stand up to Charles V, no decisive actions could be taken.

Christmas at Greenwich that year was a most interesting affair. As official queen, Catherine was in attendance. As betrothed to the king, so was Anne. Confused visitors and dignitaries paid equal respects to both hostesses.

News reached Henry in February of 1529 that Pope Clement VII had died. In such an event, Cardinal Wolsey would undoubtedly succeed Clement and take care of Henry's annulment dilemma. Regrettably, Clement was still alive and more afraid of Charles V than ever.

Emboldened by her nephew the emperor's support, Catherine demanded a trial in Rome, where she planned to summon Henry for questioning. Henry responded that if she continued to plot against him, he would separate her from her daughter Mary. At the same time, Anne wrote a letter to the king's agent in Rome, Gardiner, and asked him for new papal orders permitting the annulment. The lack of response greatly annoyed Henry.

It became impossible to delay the trial any further. The pope's representative, Campeggio, and Henry first minister, Wolsey, took their seats in the great hall of the monastery of the Black Friars to preside over Henry's annulment in the summer of 1529. An excited and divided England awaited the outcome.

Catherine, now plump with middle-age, headed straight for Henry and knelt. Declaring that she had been a dutiful wife, she pleaded with him to spare her this humiliation. She left the room without waiting for a response. Henry reaffirmed that he believed the marriage was a sin and asked for the court to agree to an annulment. Still, no decision was made. For several weeks, Wolsey visited Catherine and pleaded with her to change her mind. It was a fruitless effort; she insisted she would never give up her rightful place as queen to a whore.

While the legal rambling continued, supporters for both sides brought up different parts of the Bible to prove their case. Henry insisted he was not a married man and free to wed anyone he chose. Still, once he married Anne and they had a child, the child's legitimacy could not be brought into question—he needed to wait until the marriage to Catherine was officially declared invalid before begetting the all-important heir. Time was running out. Anne was nearing her 30th birthday, middle-aged in those days.

While defying the pope directly was a possibility, it meant certain excommunication. This was a step that frightened even a king such as Henry and one which he was not yet prepared to take. Frustrated, he blamed Rome for refusing to cooperate. This was a public humiliation. Since Wolsey had initially been ordered to deal with the pope, Henry blamed him for the failure to procure an annulment. Caught between a frightened pope and an angry king, Wolsey knew his future at court was uncertain. Henry now appointed the Lutheran Thomas Cromwell to the Privy Council to continue procuring his annulment.

Chapter Six

The King's Great Matter

"If it ever lay in my power, I will work the Cardinal as much displeasure as he has done to me."

—Anne Boleyn about Cardinal Wolsey

Although Pope Clement VII was clearly reluctant to involve himself in what was referred to as the "King's Great Matter," Anne blamed Cardinal Wolsey for delaying and hindering the annulment.

Due to the power of Emperor Charles V, all of Europe now became enmeshed in Henry's private affairs. With the Treaty of Cambrai, Charles gathered all of Henry's enemies against him. The emperor also sent Eustace Chapuys to London to serve as the imperial ambassador. For seven years, Chapuys spied on the English court and sent information back to Charles, specifically information relating to Catherine and her daughter, Mary.

Chapuys became one of Catherine's greatest supporters and remained devoted to her throughout the rest of her life. He hated Anne, and all of his reports to the emperor were filled with insults about the "whore" or "concubine," as he called her. He placed his spies everywhere. Although he never once met Anne, he no doubt referenced Catherine's own language when referring to the younger woman. At any opportunity, Chapuys spreads vicious lies about Anne to anyone who would listen. He became one of her worst enemies at court.

With their relationship out in the open, Anne joined Henry on his summer progress, although still not his bed. Upon their return to London, a frustrated Campeggio returned to Rome due to lack of any progress. Henry had him followed. He had heard that Wolsey had placed a spy with Campeggio to take Anne's secret letters to Henry back to the pope. Wolsey was still desperately hoping for evidence that could be used to smear Anne. Campeggio was stopped at Dover, and the letters were indeed found in his possession. None of the letters contained any suggestion that Anne was or had ever been Henry's mistress. They were perfectly harmless.

Henry's patience with Wolsey was waning. For his deception, Wolsey was forced to leave his London home, York Place, and dismissed as chancellor, but he still escaped prison—for the time being. He was replaced as chancellor by Thomas More, a fanatic opponent of the Reformation.

The confiscation of Wolsey's fabulous palaces helped stir up considerable anti-Rome sentiments among the population. These properties, York Place (later renamed Whitehall Palace) and Hampton Court, were grander than most of the king's residences and rivaled Versailles in splendor. Wolsey had accumulated a fortune and loved to show off his wealth. The populace began to wonder just how much money clerics were taking in. The fact was bishops, cardinals, and other clerics charged hefty fees for everything. With the corruption of Rome brought to light, many English citizens saw the move away from the papacy as the best possible future for England. For Anne, this subtle move away from Rome could only be good news.

Theologian Thomas Cranmer and George Boleyn discussed the radical idea that Henry was under the sole authority of God, not Rome. Cranmer suggested the matter be placed not with lawmakers, but with other learned theologians. Henry enthusiastically agreed.

By this point, Henry treated Anne like the future queen of England in every way but marriage. He gifted her with every possible extravagance, including expensive linens for her underwear. After Wolsey was forced to vacate York Place, Henry had it especially renovated for Anne as her own, private residence. But Anne was growing impatient. Hadn't she been waiting for seven years? With her 30th birthday approaching, she lashed out at the king: "I have been waiting long, and might in the meantime have contracted some advantageous marriage, out of which I might have had issue . . . But alas! Farewell to my time and youth spent to no purpose at all!"

Her ire was certainly understandable. She, Catherine, and Henry were living in a strange *ménage à trois*. Catherine was still attending official functions at court in her capacity as queen, while Anne was also in attendance as a kind of queen-in-waiting. It was a confusing situation for everyone. Henry himself wasn't getting any younger. He was gaining weight, losing hair, and the sores on his legs were becoming more pronounced. While working on his annulment, he had grown into an old man.

No one had expected the "King's Matter" to stretch out over years and involve most of Europe. Catherine and her nephew, Emperor Charles V, were proving fiercer and more stubborn than anyone could have anticipated. The pope, still living under Charles's domination, was forbidding Henry to marry anyone under pains of excommunication. So far, Catherine was still playing her winning card to win. But how long could she remain in the game?

As for Henry, he desperately hoped that an annulment was still a possibility. Otherwise, he was turning into the laughingstock of Europe.

Chapter Seven
Anne Ascends the Throne

"She is my death, and I am hers."

—Anne Boleyn about Catherine of Aragon

The ménage à trois was finally dissolved when Catherine was removed permanently from court to Hertfordshire in 1531. Her surroundings were comfortable, but she continued to complain about her deprivations. She raged at Henry's demand to return all royal jewels. The emperor's ambassador, Chapuys, kept her apprised of all happenings at court. Reporting to the emperor, he falsely wrote, "Lady Anne is hated by all the world."

Fifteen-year-old Mary, who by now had been declared illegitimate, was sent to her cousin Margaret Douglas to live and to be schooled. Since Henry was extremely wary of what he saw as Catherine's continued plotting against him with Charles V, he tried to keep mother and daughter apart.

The pope continued to send messages that Henry needed to rid himself of Anne and take Catherine back. This only served to infuriate the king. Standing up to Rome and facing the possibility of excommunication was not something Henry wanted to do. But he was desperate to end this long, drawn-out drama. Taking Anne's advice, he finally decided that the pope had no power over England.

He cut off revenues to the papacy and announced his right to appoint his own bishops and cardinals without the pope's approval. Politely, he informed the pope that it was his citizens who were demanding these changes. In a final snub to the Pope, Henry now proclaimed himself "Protector and Supreme Head of the Church of England." In protest, Chancellor Thomas More immediately resigned as chief minister the following day.

The power of the papacy in England was being dismantled slowly but surely. With the catholic Wolsey out of the way, Thomas Cranmer was rising in the ranks and was finally appointed archbishop of Canterbury in 1532. Thomas Cromwell, alongside Cranmer, was charged with putting an end to the long wait. Clear battle lines were being drawn.

When Henry traveled to meet Francis I of France, royal protocol was tossed on its head. What was he to do with Anne? Francis even offered to keep his own wife, Queen Claude, at home and bring his maîtresse en titre to the meeting, but being placed on par with a mistress was seen as an insult to Anne. Eventually, the two monarchs met without any women while the ladies had a meeting of their own. Anne was clearly regarded as the head of the female delegation. King Francis even sent her diamonds worth a fortune.

Perhaps it was this acceptance from European royalty that led Anne to Henry's bed for the first time in their years-long courtship. They finally became lovers in Calais. Some chroniclers report that a secret marriage took place at that time. Wherever the marriage took place, Henry and Anne now considered themselves man and wife. Anne immediately fulfilled her destiny by becoming pregnant. No one's joy could have been greater than Henry's. To ensure the baby's legitimacy, Henry and Anne remarried in January 1533 upon their return to England in York Place in front of witnesses, although the marriage was kept a secret from the public.

After nine long years, Anne was finally queen of England. But, so was Catherine. The English realm now officially had two queens. It was Anne, however, who attended Easter Services with the king as queen of England. Their marriage was announced to one and all. Officially, Catherine was now referred to as the dowager queen. Having little choice at this point, Parliament decreed that Henry's marriage to Catherine had never been legal. Anne was recognized as his one and only true wife.

Queen Anne was triumphantly paraded through London and given a joyous welcome. Many Londoners had been questioning the pope's hold over their king and approved of the split between England and Rome. The reformed religion was slowly infiltrating England, although Thomas More was working hard at squelching these new heretical ideas. Above all else, after over 20 years, the arrival of an heir was anticipated with tremendous joy. Anne waved at the crowd with equal enthusiasm. Her plan at age 20 had been to make a successful marriage. She had finally achieved her dreams and goals.

Not everyone, however, felt hopeful. The pope was infuriated at this defiance. He immediately excommunicated Henry. Henry, eagerly awaiting the birth of his son, ignored the pope. Henry was so convinced that he would beget a son that he had all official papers prepared beforehand.

For her confinement, Anne was taken to Greenwich with tremendous ceremony. It was a time when childbirth was a great risk to both mother and child. All of England prayed fervently for their safety and good health. Anne gave birth to the long-awaiting child on September 7, 1533, but it was a girl. Everyone pretended to be happy. Both Henry and Anne tried to disguise their disappointment, while scribes quickly changed all of the official papers which had already been prepared to announce a son.

The girl was named Elizabeth. She was christened on September 10. Her 17-year-old half-sister, Mary, was immediately disinherited. Chapuys, still attempting to create dissent, wrote to his master Charles V that he should invade England and reinstate Catherine.

Anne wanted to keep Elizabeth close. Henry, however, sent her away at three months to her own household. Anne was devasted, but clearly, Henry had little interest in another daughter and didn't want her close-by. By Christmas, Anne was again pregnant. This time, hopefully, it would be a son. She had proven herself fertile, so it was just a matter of time. Feeling secure in her new position, Anne appointed chaplains of the new religion to her household, helping to keep the Reformation in the forefront. She did much charity work and was generally liked by the people, Chapuys' claims notwithstanding.

Henry's natural cruel streak showed itself when he appointed his daughter Mary as an attendant to her half-sister Elizabeth. Catherine, who was not permitted to see Mary, wrote to her daughter and told her to defy her father and repudiate Anne and Elizabeth. Henry considered this sheer treason. Fifty years of sisterly rivalry was set in motion.

Chapter Eight

Another Birth, Another Tragedy

"Am I not a man like any other?"

—Henry VIII to Eustace Chapuys

The following year, Anne's second pregnancy resulted in a miscarriage. Henry's quest for a son was dealt another severe blow, and questions as to the king's virility were raised. Henry would have six wives and many mistresses. Yet only four of these women conceived with him. People began to wonder if lack of conception for 20 years had really been Catherine's fault. Henry experienced recurring bladder problems and might have suffered from syphilis. Anne herself wrote about his "lack of strength." Henry and King Francis I shared several mistresses (including Anne's sister Mary), and Francis was known to have a severe case of syphilis. Henry, of course, would never acknowledge any problem. He simply traded old wives for new ones. He could not be the source of the difficulties.

Chapuys continued his spread of disinformation, which, actually, was his job as Charles V's spymaster. When Princess Mary fell ill, he convinced her Anne was trying to poison her.

In 1534, Clement died and was succeeded by Pope Paul III. This raised hopes in certain quarters that Rome and England might once again become reconciled. However, Paul III's first act was to confirm Henry's excommunication. The new reformed religion was causing riots and killings in France as mobs took to the streets in revolt. The Catholics in France lauded the new pope's actions and declared Anne to be a fraudulent wife. This would make Elizabeth illegitimate and ruin her chances in the European marriage market. Francis I's own sister, a Protestant, had to flee to Navarre to save her life.

For Henry and Anne, the need for another child, a son, made the state of their marriage even more critical. To observers, their relationship was filled with tension. Henry declared any acknowledgment of papal powers to be treason. Refusing to accept Henry as the Head of the Church of England was punishable by death. Cromwell supported him fully in this separation from Rome.

Anne was no fool. She knew her very life depended upon the fact that Henry remained in love with her. How safe was she if she couldn't provide him with the son he wanted? It must have crossed her mind that Henry would value an heir more than he valued her.

Henry and Anne's honeymoon period soon came to a harsh end. Much to Henry's consternation, Anne suffered a second miscarriage. Her miscarriages were becoming too reminiscent of Catherine's own losses. Anne had every right to be nervous—the couple had more problems ahead.

While there had been some sympathy throughout Europe during Henry's struggle for an annulment, his complete break with Rome appalled most. These anti-

English feelings were encouraged by Charles V, who continued to receive messages regarding Catherine's suffering from Chapuys. There was even a conspiracy to depose Henry and replace the English king with his first daughter, Mary.

When ex-Chancellor More refused to support Henry, Henry had him executed. The emperor's fleet had reached the mouth of the Thames, ready to attack. Now that Charles had repelled the Islamic forces attempting to invade Europe for the second time, Henry had his full attention. Nothing would have pleased Catherine more than England being invaded. Everyone was holding their breath.

Catherine's death January 7, 1536, most likely prevented a full-scale war. Henry's response to her death was, "God be praised that we are free from all suspicion of war!" Anne wrote Mary a letter promising she would be a "second mother" to the child. Mary refused even to respond. Her mother and Chapuys had taught the young girl to hate Anne.

Anne miscarried another child in 1536 who appeared to be male. Her relationship with Henry became extremely tense. Clearly, Anne was not fulfilling her end of the marriage bargain. According to Henry, "I was deceived into this marriage by sorcery . . . I believe I could take another wife." The statement that he'd been deceived into marriage was somewhat disingenuous, considering how long Henry had pursued Anne. But it boded of an ill wind on the horizon.

Since Henry could never admit to having any fertility problems, Anne carried all of the blame for the latest loss. The thought of another wife was foremost on his mind. For

Henry, any woman who could provide him with a son would do. He began publicly pursuing pretty little Jane Seymour, who had been one of Catherine's ladies-in-waiting and now served Anne. History strangely repeated itself. Henry first courted Anne while Anne was a lady-in-waiting to Catherine. Now, Henry began courting Jane Seymour, who was a lady-in-waiting to Anne, a second wife who also seemed unable to bear him sons.

As he had with Anne, Henry showered Jane with gifts. She kept the gifts but returned the money he gave her. She enjoyed showing off a pendant with Henry's picture around her neck. Anne once snatched the pendant from her with considerable force. Both women apparently came to blows frequently.

Jane's family, seeing an opportunity for their own betterment, encouraged this new romance. Everyone at court could see that Anne was on her way out. For years, Henry had admired Anne's intelligence and had followed her lead in religious matters. Now, he became irritated at her confidence and intellect, telling her that this was not the way a true wife behaved. Jane Seymour, who could barely read and write, looked good in comparison. Jane never argued and agreed with whatever the king said.

Over the years, Anne had made plenty of enemies at court who resented her for usurping Catherine and for her support of the Protestant religion. These enemies, including the ever-present Chapuys, were more than happy to push this malleable Jane Seymour at the king and bring about Anne's ruin. Like the Boleyns before, the Seymours were now anticipating good fortunes through a royal marriage.

Jane's parents and brothers encouraged her relationship with the king, and she happily obliged.

The king's new romance was not carried out with discretion. Henry made a specific point of being with Jane when Anne was in the same room. Jane paraded his gifts of jewelry to one and all and spoke of the king's devotion to her. It was clear that Henry now wanted to get rid of Anne as much as he had previously wanted to rid himself of Catherine. The first hint that the Boleyns were falling out of favor was that George, Anne's brother, was not to be initiated into the Order of the Garter, as had been long expected. The Catholics at court were gleefully whispering about there being a "change in the air."

Henry looked to Thomas Cromwell, who had helped him get rid of Catherine, to now do the same with Anne. Cromwell had witnessed Wolsey's downfall when the cardinal had failed to secure Henry with an annulment. Cromwell knew that unless he succeeded in pleasing the king, he would meet the same fate. Getting rid of Anne became his obsession in order to save his own position. Cromwell knew Henry to be a petty man. For Cromwell, it was either his fate or Queen Anne's. He was determined that he would not lose. Anne had to go—regardless of any information he had to invent to achieve that purpose.

Cromwell's first step was to coordinate his efforts with Chapuys, Anne's longtime enemy. The Catholic spymaster and the ambitious Protestant courtier were working as a team toward a common goal. Most of Europe was on their side if it meant returning England to the Catholic fold. Charges of adultery on Anne's part were discussed—regardless of the fact that Henry was shamelessly flaunting his affair with Jane Seymour at court. Henry himself pretended to be ignorant of any plans regarding Anne.

Anne feared for her and her daughter's life for good reason. The man who had professed his undying love for a decade was now turning against her. He had destroyed one wife, what would prevent him from destroying another? He had defied the world by marrying Anne in order to create a son. She had failed him in the exact same way Catherine had. Now, once again, he was turning into a laughingstock. All he had to show for his efforts was another barren wife and puny daughter. There still was no heir in sight. As far as Henry was concerned, Anne had betrayed him.

When Henry unexpectedly called Parliament into session, Anne knew it was bad news. She confronted him but was met with anger and derision. Mentally, Henry was already rid of wife number two. All that was lacking were the particulars to make it happen. In the meantime, Cromwell was hard at work gathering information that could be used to destroy the queen. He arranged for spies everywhere, including Anne's private apartments. He bribed her ladies generously for any information that could bring harm to Anne. It didn't matter whether the information was true or false. Rumors soon began to circulate. According to the spies, Anne was seen entertaining gentlemen in her private chambers. They assured Cromwell that they could produce witnesses to the queen's affairs. The worst of the rumors being spread was that Anne had been seeing kissing her own brother, George, and that she was probably pregnant by him.

Those preparing for Anne's trial first considered a charge of treason, which was punishable by death. But treason was far more difficult to prove than adultery. For a charge of adultery, all Cromwell had to do was line up sufficient and appropriate witnesses. He gathered the names of five men who had allegedly enjoyed the queen's favors. As Cromwell later pointed out in court, not even a virile man such as Henry could satisfy the passions of an evil woman such as Anne.

No statement was too absurd to prove that Anne, who had spent seven years avoiding Henry's bed, was now entertaining any number of men in her own. Henry and Anne had been married approximately one thousand days. What had started in bliss would end in sheer, bloody tragedy.

Chapter Nine

Trial and Execution

"Good Christian People, I have not come here to preach a sermon; I have come here to die."

—Anne Boleyn

All the evidence against Anne was amassed within a week. Henry wanted the whole sordid affair over and done with as quickly as possible. Her trial took place on May 15, 1536, in the Tower of London, less than two weeks following her arrest. She was accused of conspiracy against the king and carnal knowledge of several men, including her brother.

The men Cromwell had selected were Henry Norris, Francis Weston, artist Mark Smeaton, William Brereton, and George Boleyn, Anne's brother. Strangely, every so-called "carnal meeting" was presented with two dates, as if Anne had slept with these men twice each and then discarded them. The court completely ignored the fact that Anne, a queen and never alone, had alibis for most of the dates given. Additionally, it was suggested that one of these men was actually Elizabeth's true father. Anne's flirtatious nature, learned at the French court, made it easy to accuse and condemn her for lewd behavior.

As for an incestuous relationship with George, the court claimed, Anne "tempted her brother with her tongue in the said George's mouth and the said George's tongue in hers."

Evidence against George came from his wife, Jane, who was in an unhappy marriage and likely jealous of her sister-in-law, the queen. Providing testimony against her husband was the most convenient way of ridding herself of an unwanted husband. Jane would later be executed herself for high treason.

Any innocent moment of Anne's life was taken out of context and presented as proof of adultery. Presenting courtiers with money or dancing with George, common enough occurrences, were twisted into something lewd and sinful. It was hinted that Anne was a witch, because who else but such an evil woman could hold the attention of the king for so many years?

None of those on trial were provided with counsel or were allowed to speak. Everyone knew what the outcome would be. All witnesses were subsequently linked to Cromwell. To muddy the waters, several witnesses were produced to declare that Anne had promised to marry Henry Norris following Henry's death, which added the charge of treason against her. George Boleyn and all the other men, except the artist Smeaton, proclaimed their innocence. Under torture, Smeaton confessed he did indeed have an affair with Anne.

The presiding found Anne guilty of all charges. The punishment would be either burning at the stake or beheading. Anne's response to this verdict was, "I do not say that I have always borne towards the King the humility which I owed him, considering his kindness and the great honor he showed me and the great respect he always paid me; I admit too, that often I have taken it into my head to be jealous of him. But God knows, and is my witness, that I've not sinned against him in any other way."

Her brother George and the other four men were also found guilty. They were executed on May 17; Anne watched the spectacle from the Tower.

There is no doubt that this trial was planned by Cromwell and Chapuys. The verdict was a foregone conclusion, already dictated by Henry. Henry revealed to Jane Seymour that Anne would be condemned before the trial even started. So sure was he of the outcome, he was already planning his next wedding. Cromwell and Chapuys may have orchestrated the trial, but Henry was clearly giving the orders. Anne had failed to provide him with a son. This betrayal could not be forgiven.

Following the guilty verdict, Anne was kept as a prisoner in the Tower. The Tower of London at the time was not only a prison but a place of royal celebrations. Ironically, Anne had been feted and dined here on several occasions by the king. Now, it would serve as her final place of confinement. The Tower Green was the site of the lethal scaffold that would behead her. Catherine Howard, Henry's fifth wife, would meet her end in the same place a few years later.

After two nights in the Tower, on May 19, 1536, Anne and her ladies made their way from their rooms to the scaffold. A crowd was already in place to witness her beheading. She went up the steps and faced her executioner bravely. Her execution had happened so quickly, no one had planned a funeral for the former queen. Although she spent her time in the Tower praying, even she was unprepared for her quick end. Her ladies wrapped her body and severed head in a white cloth and carried her to the Chapel of St. Peter. She was buried in an unmarked grave within the chapel. The grave, now marked, receives millions of visitors every year. Many still debate whether Anne was a whore or a martyr. No one, however, can deny that she was fascinating and brave.

In the days following Anne's execution, Henry married his third wife, Jane Seymour. His daughter Elizabeth was declared illegitimate, just like Mary had been. All traces of Anne's existence were removed; no letters or paintings remain.

The year following her marriage to Henry, Jane Seymour finally gave Henry the son he craved. Jane herself died in childbirth. Henry married three more times in an effort to secure his succession, but he would have no more children. His only legitimate son, Edward VI, died at age 15, leaving Mary to inherit the crown as the first English queen to rule in her own right.

Conclusion

Anne Boleyn is certainly the best-known of Henry's many wives, and she remains the source of much fascination and speculation. Anne left a legacy of tragedy due to her inability to provide the king with a son—frequently overlooked are her contributions in bringing Protestantism to England and removing England from the power of the papacy. She took tremendous risks in helping bring banned books across the Channel into England.

The new faith was gaining influence throughout England, although Queen Mary I, Catherine of Aragon's daughter, tried to reinstate Catholicism and ban the new books. She never forgave Anne for the pain caused to herself and her mother and grew bitter and hateful. A zealous Catholic like her mother, Mary refused to accept the reformed religion and burned at the stake those who did. Thomas Cranmer, one of Anne's most loyal supporters, was one of the first to meet his fate by being burned. Mary's bitterness extended to her half-sister, Elizabeth, whom she refused to name as her heir.

Anne Boleyn's daughter, Queen Elizabeth I, did take the crown and upheld and helped strengthen the reformed religion, which remains England's main religion to this day. Elizabeth I grew up to become one of England's greatest monarchs, ruling over the realm for 44 years. Elizabeth was merely four years old when Anne died. Elizabeth never spoke of her. However, following her death in 1603, a ring she had on her finger for 25 years was discovered to contain a miniature painting of Anne with Elizabeth as an infant.

Elizabeth never married, even though her need for an heir was as dire as her father's had been. She was the final ruler of the Tudor line which both Henry VII and VIII had fought so hard to maintain and for which they had killed so many people. Was Elizabeth loathe to share her powers, or was Henry VIII's example as a husband enough to convinced her to choose the single life? Certainly, Henry's cruel behavior toward each of his six wives has earned him the reputation as a deplorable king and husband.

Whatever can be said about Anne Boleyn, her life was colorful and memorable, and her death served to reveal the true horror dispensed to wives who displeased their royal husbands.

Made in the USA
Monee, IL
23 October 2023